You Could Be the Problem

Darrin Huff
You Could Be the Problem

Published by Spines
ISBN: 979-8-89383-053-8

You Could Be the Problem

Dating in the Modern Era

Darrin Huff

CONTENTS

Acknowledgments

I would like to thank my friends and co-workers for the motivation in helping me write my book. They were all amazing in helping me temper my feelings. I can be very passionate on this topic and can at times loose focus. Lol

I also would like to thank my son Darrin and my daughter Denae for being so amazing and making me the most proud father. This book is my way of sharing with them my insights on dating and how to avoid the most common mistakes while dating. My babies walk your life as you see fit and know that your dad is very proud of you and I am so very proud to have you as my children.

Introduction

In this day and age, I have noticed that there is a huge divide between men and women in the dating world. There have been a lot of conversations on TikTok, Facebook, and on all the other social media platforms about how dating has changed. So, I just wanted to give my two cents.

With the advice of friends whom I have shared my dating experience with, they had urged me to put my thoughts to paper. Please take my opinions with a grain of salt. I am not talking to everyone because this does not apply to everyone.

My writing is focused on reaching people who are tired of getting the same old results and don't know why. People who are sick and tired of being sick and tired.

Now, my thoughts may trigger a lot of people, and if they do, then you should ask yourself why. I don't know you, and I did not mention any names at all. So why are you triggered? Could it be because you have heard, read, experienced, or even talked about this subject and are still unable to get the results that you want? It could be you love being the victim and want to cry to anyone who is willing to listen. Well, guess what? No one cares!

No one cares because this is a YOU problem and not an us problem. You are not a victim. You are a product of your own insecurities. You are experiencing the results of your bad decisions and never learning from them. What you are is a misunderstood person who just needs therapy. Stop blaming everyone and everything for your problems. Look in a mirror; you have created your own problems, not God, your momma, your daddy, your auntie, not your boss, not your co-worker. It's all you. So, in order to find better, you must become a better version of yourself.

So, I hope that my insights will help you to choose better and to get out of your own way.

You can do it.

CHAPTER 1

NO ONE CARES

I have talked with a lot of men and women about dating. The common theme is "all" men and women ain't shit. When I first heard this, I was like you ain't never lied. I had just reentered the dating market after being married for 15 years. So, the first thing I did after taking a few months to get my head together was to get back into the dating market.

At first, I thought this should be pretty cool. There are a lot of women who are looking for a decent guy. It shouldn't take me that long to find someone. LOL Boy, was I delusional. Seven years later, I had come to the realization that dating apps are garbage. When I say garbage, I mean that I was not able to make a meaningful connection with anyone. Dating apps can and do work for a lot of people. I just wasn't one of them. So, I decided to try something different. I decided to try a professional matchmaker. My thought was that in order to get a different result that, maybe I should try a different method. I knew the type of woman that I was looking for was special. So, maybe she might be trying the same thing. Nope, it didn't matter. It wasn't that I was using the wrong app or looking in the wrong places. The problem was that most of the women who were out in these streets were not worth the effort.

When I was on the dating app, I did find two people whom I wanted to marry and had proposed to. I later had to reject both of them. This is when I had to ask myself why I was meeting the same person in a different body. I couldn't figure it out on my own. So, I decided to go get therapy. The sessions allowed me to see things more clearly. With this clarity, I came to the realization that this generation of women is not looking for a relationship. They are looking for a lifestyle with entitlement. The funny thing is, regardless of their age, they all seemed to be acting like spoiled, argumentative, entitled children.

Now, upon reflection on all of my encounters. I realized that the problem is the fact that most women fail to take accountability and responsibility for their past and present actions. They choose poorly and then blame the men that they have chosen and chased after for not being the man that they really want. Yeah, ladies, this really sounds like a YOU problem.

The guy's major problem is that they have become so numb to the process that they would rather either just stop looking or go overseas to find someone. These are the types of guys who have put in the work and know what they are looking for. These are the good guys (more on him later). The problem with this action is that once you bring them back to the U.S., she will become Westernized, and all of the virtue she had when you first met will go out the window.

Men in the pursuit of qualifying for a better-quality woman. We need to become better men. We become better men by:

- Become physically fit.
- Get a job that can support a family.
- Surround yourself with men with similar goals.
- Stop making excuses for your shortcomings.

So, it is not that there are not any good men or women out here anymore. The reality is that you have not put in the work to be with the type of person you want.

Ladies, to get the man that you want. You must put in some type of work.

Just to be clear, the bare minimum:

- Be fit – The ability to execute daily activities with optimal performance, endurance and strength with the management of disease, fatigue, and stress and reduce sedentary behavior.
- Be friendly – Kind and pleasant.

CHAPTER 2

REMEMBER BACK IN THE DAY

Remember when you were a young man full of optimism? The very thought of having a girlfriend was exciting. The very first time you asked her out on a date. This was your first time acting as a man. You were making a decision that would affect someone other than yourself. How exciting it was seeing your mom's face smiling at you as you were cheesing from ear to ear at the news. The proud look your father beamed seeing his son entering manhood. Remember the first time you had to deal with meeting her mom and dad? How nervous were you? It's funny now when you think back. You have known her family for years, but now that you are going on a date. Her father was acting like this was the first time you have ever met him. LOL, and in a way, it was. This will be the first time that you are no longer being seen as children but as a young adult.

You will now be trying to figure out how much money you are going to need. Taking on the responsibility of planning the entire date. The first time that you make a conscious decision to watch your surroundings because trouble can come up at any time. You had to always be on guard. This was your first journey into learning how to be a protector. As a young man, learning how to make a good impression by opening the door for her, paying for the meals, and not arguing in public. You were focused on her the entire time. Making her feel like she was the only one in your life because she was. This laid the foundations for how you would treat a woman as you get older.

Ladies, remember how you felt on your first date. The first time you told your mom that you were going out on a date. How she gave you that look like "really" well I hope that you have a good time. How your father, on the other hand, was like you are getting ready to do "WHAT?" Go on a "WHAT?" Who is he, and where did you meet him? Let me check him out. Your mother had to jump in and say go on your date and have fun. I will handle your father. LOL, these are the memories we had when we were young and innocent. As a young lady, this will be your first time seeing him not as just a friend but as a young man who is trying to impress you. Now, he is the same guy that you have always known, but it feels different. You are looking at him differently. You are now seeing him as a provider and protector for the very first time. You were so nervous and anxious. Not knowing what to expect or really how you feel things should go. As a young lady, you see him in a different light and wonder, wow, this is it, just like in the movies.

These are the experiences we had growing up. I know that you are still smiling when you think about these times. It was so innocent and new that was then.

CHAPTER 3

WELCOME TO REALITY TV DATING

There are four basic types of reality shows: the dating, the celebrity marriage, the gaming and the culture fusion reality.

Reality dating has become very popular, where women expect the world without contributing anything. In these dating streets, the average women with children are expecting a man whom they have just met to not only pay for her meals but also buy enough for her children. Where they expect a man to pay for dates that cost over two hundred dollars because they spent money on their hair and nails for the date, so you can't just hangout out more it has to be a whole production. Men who make over 100K are the only type of man to be considered for a date because, in her mind, if you are not making that much, then you can't afford to date.

Women have become so delusional that an online app was created called Female Delusion Calculator (you can google it; it's free). This app is to show women that it is okay to have your wants, but the reality of you finding him is slim to none. Yes, it has gotten that bad.

Look, all I am saying here is that modern women feel like there is nothing wrong with having wants. They look at reality TV, movies and social media and think what they are seeing is real. They see women posting how they met a guy who did this and that and think yes, that could be me. Is it possible that you could run into a guy who does this or that? Sure, it is possible, just not probable. Ladies' social media is not real. It is driven by clicks and likes. Most podcasters' entire show is geared to trigger an emotional response from you. The podcaster will say and do whatever it takes to get subscribers and likes.

Why in the world would you take advice from anyone who:

- You don't know.
- Who divorced their spouse because of what they did and then cried? Victim.
- Who can't keep a healthy relationship?
- Has multiple children by different men or women.
- Entertainers who either don't have a man, can't keep a man or settle for a man they know is not their first or second choice but will choose him because she doesn't want to be alone.
- Or take advice from artists who sing that man ain't shit yet they are married.
- Who blames men for all the bad things that have happened to them yet ignores

the fact that they were the ones who chased after them?

Why would you rather take advice from women or men on social media? Who did the same shit that you did, ended up where you are and think you will get better than them? Girl, please, you are not delusional. You are crazy. You know first-hand how some people are. They can be very petty and jealous. They will talk behind your back and try to sabotage the good thing that you have going on because they can't get what you have found. They have become so bitter, angry, and frustrated, yet you honestly think they will wish the best for you? Come on now. This is social media that we are talking about.

Now, we do have some really good content creators whom I would consider you to take a look at. These are men and women who are fighting for you. Men and women who are calling out bad behavior. They are giving you a point of view that can help you change your life. Information that could help you become the better version of yourself. They could lead you to a relationship that would be healthy for you. You may not like the delivery or the tone, but you need to focus on the message. My list could have been larger, but I will leave it up to you to find whom you would rather follow.

My starter list is on YouTube:

- I would recommend:
- Rivah Tv

- Pink Book Lessons
- Crimson Cure
- DeeDee
- D'Nieka Marie Dope Discussions
- @whatever Podcast
- Mediocre Tutorials and Reviews
- Manosphere Highlights
- The Crucible
- Moa Podcast

So, now the question becomes, who are you looking for? What type of man or woman would be a good fit for you, and what are they looking for?

CHAPTER 4

WHAT TYPE OF MAN ARE YOU?

There are different types of men in this world. They are:

- The Traditional Man
- The Good guy
- The Pookie
- The Ray-Ray
- The Brad and Chad
- The Bad boy
- The Simp

In this era, a traditional man is glamorized and demonized at the same time. Most women say that they want a traditional man but don't even know what that means. So, let's take a little time to explore.

The Traditional Man:

- A leader.
- The main Breadwinner.

- The protector.
- Ever responsible.
- Provides emotional support.
- A good communicator while showing respect and consideration.
- Faithful to the commitment towards each other.
- The problem Solver.

This is what the modern woman fantasizes about: the gold standard that all men are supposed to aspire to become. The only problem is no man on this planet has ever been this guy. He was created by Disney, Media outlets, Hollywood, Romance novels and advertisers. Women love to throw this image in men's faces whenever they can. They know this person does not exist, and even if he did, they would not want him. Hell, the moment he tries to tell her anything, it's a wrap. She is back to the streets. No man is going to tell her what to do.

The Good Guy

· *Good guy* – Typically means that the person being referred to is considered to be kind, trustworthy, and generally positive in their behavior and character.

The Good Guy is usually the guy who is in most women's friend zones. He is the guy who is dependable and has most of the traits of a traditional man. He is your blue, white-collar worker. Who works a regular 9 to 5? He only drinks or smokes socially. You don't usually find him out in the clubs. He is usually out in the community trying to make a difference. He will cater to a woman's emotional needs without any expectations of appreciation. He will be willing to be a role model to her children, who are not his own. He will volunteer to be a part of a mentorship program. He doesn't judge anyone in need and tries to help out in any way that he can. He has traditional values and believes in the traditional roles of a man and woman.

Believe it or not, there really aren't any major differences between a good guy and a bad boy. The real difference is their long-term goals and expectations. The good guy is looking to build for the future. He is planning and researching the best jobs available to achieve the end goal. The bad boy, on the other hand, is only thinking about the present, making money any way he can. He doesn't normally work a nine-to-five. If he does, he treats the job like a part-time not a full-time position. He is always on the grind looking for the quick buck. He has no expectations for tomorrow. Women are attracted to him because he lives his life with little care, which feeds the chaotic nature that they have. Each day is a different challenge. His cash flow is always high, but when it goes low. He shows no care in the world because he feels like life is meant to be lived on the edge. When you compare the two, you can easily see that they are the same person. Just working hard for different results.

The Pookie and Ray-Ray

· ***Pookie and Ray Ray*** – a generalized, broad term that describes societal nonconformists, usually ex-convicts, jobless, unfaithful, "ghetto" dregs, incapable of social graces, commitment or gainful employment: the absentee father "baby daddy" of unwed mothers, the inmate population, the drug dealers and hustlers on the streets.

They are the average guys that you see around any neighborhood. They are the guys who are just chillin not taking life too seriously. They never took school too seriously. They usually come from all walks of life. They are not trying to excel at anything just trying to make ends meet. They can be a good asset to the community. They really are good people; they just have no real ambition. I think of them as good guys who just lack ambition.

The Bad Boy

·***The Bad Boy*** – a man who does not conform to approved standards of behavior, especially in a particular sphere of activity.

They are the most desired by women in their teens to mid-thirties. They are the elite in manhood to all the women in the streets. These are the men that their momma used to date. He is the father of her children. He is the one who comes home whenever he wants. Has a few side chicks around the way. He has the swag of I don't give a fuck. He is always ready for a fight. He could be a drug dealer or a cashier at a grocery store. He could work in the post office or even be a police officer. He is the type of man who could sit in a board room or in a bar room shooting pool. He has a presence of authority without any rules.

Brad and Chad

· *Brad and Chad* - are College-age males who are arrogant, self-aggrandizing a frat bro. He is the more educated version of the bad boy persona. They are the stereotypical alpha male who is attractive, successful, muscular, cocky, and very popular.

These are the cream of the crop for women. These guys have the potential to achieve whatever they set their minds to do. They have the family structure and the drive. Women watch these guys all through college to see if they are making the right moves to become the best version of themselves. They believe that these guys will be the future CEO's or Professional athletes. So they will attach themselves to them as quickly as possible. They could care less about his personality or if he cheats. They only have their eyes on the bag and are getting his attention.

The Simp

·*The Simp* – A man who throws money or attention at a woman in order to gain her affection, even when his tactics aren't working.

Now, this type of man no woman could ever respect in any way, shape, form or fashion. These are the beta men, the scavengers. They blame the world for their lack of attracting any favorable attention from women or men. They can't get a girlfriend because they have no social skills. They are in all walks of life. When trying to compensate for their lack of social skills. They lead with money. Trying to entice them, not realizing that this makes them look desperate. They are the type of people who think that Only Fans care about them. They go to a strip club and think when a stripper gives them some attention that she really likes him. They have very few male friends because they come across as being socially awkward. Now, I am calling these guys out because, my brothers, you need to work on your self-esteem. Understand that the ladies are not taking you seriously because you have nothing of value to offer them. Just giving them money with no strings attached is crazy. If you need to develop social skills, then try going to a matchmaker. They can give you constructive advice on how to do better. They have workshops and seminars that can teach you how to have better social skills. You can do better. Believe in yourself. Stop spending money on Only Fans and spend that money on bettering yourself. So that you can get a real girlfriend. The choice is yours.

CHAPTER 5

WHAT TYPE OF WOMAN ARE YOU?

What are the different types of women in this world? They are:

- The Keeper / Trophy Wife.
- Someone to play with / Dating Girlfriend.
- For the Streets / Can't take seriously.

The Keeper/Trophy Wife - She is the most desirable. She is wife material.

She came from a two-family household. She was raised in a traditional family. She will have no children and has very few boyfriends. She has very little social media presence. She is willing to pamper her man with words of affirmation, acts of service and a nurturing nature. Now, by no means am I implying this to all two-family households. I am talking about a very specific type of household. One that has a strong father figure with leadership skills in the house. So, she was able to see how a man leads and respects his wife through the good times and bad. She was also able to see how her mom interacted with his authority and masculinity.

Now, in this household, keep an eye out on how the mom acts. This will be a strong indicator of how her daughter will treat you. This type of woman is the most highly sought-after, but she comes with high expectations. She will accept nothing less than the best from her man.

She will be looking for the type of man who can provide her with a "soft" life. She should not be responsible for paying a significant bill in the house. She is not expected to work. If she does, then it would be on a part-time basis. Her sole responsibility will be to the children and home. If you can't provide her with that lifestyle, then don't try to pursue her. Don't call her a gold digger. She is used to this type of treatment. This would be you problem, not her problem. We seem to forget that a woman this special is like gold not a diamond. Gold is good as is with no added refinement. She is best suited to be with the traditional man because she is a traditional woman.

Her qualities are:

- **Attractive** – you're beautiful enough to pull in the attention of others.
- **Discerning** – seeing and understanding clearly and intelligently.

- **Disciplined** – able to carefully control the way that you work, live, or behave, especially to achieve a goal.
- **Enthusiastic** – you show eagerness and enjoyment.
- **Supportive** - to give help or assistance or to hold something or someone up.
- **Agreeable** - pleasing to the mind or senses, especially as according well with one's tastes or needs.
- **Nurturing** - to take care of, feed, and protect someone or something, especially young children, and help them to develop.
- **Physically fit** - one's ability to execute daily activities with optimal performance, endurance, and strength with the management of disease, fatigue, and stress and reduce sedentary behavior.
- **No children**
- **Sensitive** - being kind, caring, able to pick up on the feelings of others, aware of their needs and behaving in a way that helps them feel good.
- **Sweetness** - your warmth, kindness, thoughtfulness, caring, genuine interest in something, a show of appreciation, or many other qualities you hold.
- **Gentleness** - empathic and grounded with their emotions (social intelligence), offer deep tenderness for others (love), as well as a high degree of

openness/receptivity (judgment or curiosity).

- **Warmth** - someone who comes across as friendly, open to others, enthusiastic, and affectionate.
- **Passivity** - acceptance of what happens without active response or resistance.
- **Cooperativeness** - working or acting together willingly for a common purpose or benefit.
- **Expressiveness** - the state of showing what someone thinks or feels.
- **Modesty -** having or showing a moderate or humble estimate of one's merits, importance, etc.; free from vanity, egotism, boastfulness, or great pretensions.
- **Humility** - maintaining our pride about who we are, about our achievements, about our worth – but without arrogance.
- **Empathy** - the action of understanding, being aware of, being sensitive to, and vicariously experiencing the feelings, thoughts, and experience of another of either the past or present without having the feelings, thoughts, and experience fully communicated in an objectively explicit manner.
- **Affectionate - being** warm, tender, and loving can be communicated by looks, words, gestures, or touches.

- **Kind** - being selfless, caring, compassionate, and unconditionally kind.
- **Helpful** - inclined to assist others in any situation.
- **Devotion** - great love, affection, or admiration for someone.
- **Understanding** - to be sympathetic to someone's woes.

She is looking for a man who is:

- **Emotional available** – who is emotionally honest and forthright, self-aware, someone who stays focused on her rather than a cell phone, intelligence and integrity and a feeling of being loved and desired.
- **Has respect and moral integrity** – both partners have to treat each other with respect and respect each other's opinions, careers, interests, friends, bodies and minds through their actions.
- **Has the traits of Relational Sensitivity** - Men show kindness, patience, understanding, empathy and compassion.
- **A sense of humor** – Men who have the ability to make the situation feel better than what it is.

- **Can communicate** – Being able to understand active listening and showing a sign of vulnerability.
- **Has honesty and transparency** – This is the building block for building a strong relationship.
- **Has confidence** – A man who believes in himself and knows what he wants.
- **Be a good listener** – To be able to listen to understand.

Someone to play with/Girlfriend - She is the most common that most men end up being with.

She is the type of woman who has a lot of masculine traits. She sometimes has a child out of wedlock. This child could have come from either a divorce or just bad judgment. She normally has a lot of male friends and feels more comfortable with men than women. If she does have girlfriends, they will be masculine and driven like her. She will enjoy girl trips and parting just like the men.

She is more spoiled and selfish, which is where the polishing comes in. She can become a keeper if you are willing to put in the work. In most cases, she came from the streets or a high-paying job. She can have some of the qualities as the keeper. She will not use you, but she will be watching how you spend your money. She will have her own money and is quite stable. She will be looking for a man who is making as much or more than her. You can win her over by not playing the game of show and tell. Don't show her how much money you make. Just live your life normally. Don't try to impress her. This is the fastest way to lose her interest. She is looking for someone who can match her energy.

Her typical role is management. Where she is the one who instructs and enforces company policy that requires her to take charge. This also includes jobs like nursing, lawyers, medical assistants, and police officers just to name a few. She is like a really good friend. The problem with this type of woman is that she is not used to not being in control. When she speaks, at times, she will sound condescending or even patronizing. She can, at times, make you feel like you are competing with her instead of being your peace and working with you. Don't get quickly offended. She is not even aware of her actions. She wants to be an asset to you but doesn't know how to not be in charge. Her goal is not to stress you out. She has just never thought of her behavior as being masculine or being difficult.

She could have been raised in a traditional household. The difference, being that instead of having a strong father figure. The mother was the leader. So, she feels more comfortable with taking charge instead of being submissive and supportive. She could also have been raised by a single mom. Who has learned from her mistakes? Who loves her children and does not want them to make her mistakes. Her mother would have told her about how hard it is to make it in this world without help. She would have shared that she needs to be mindful about having children outside of marriage. She would have watched and listened to her male friends and their dating experiences. So, she kinda have a better understanding of what men are looking for. What they are expecting from a relationship.

She is looking for:

- A man who has a strong personality but has a good sense of humor.
- He will have had to demonstrate that he can make good decisions as well as being able to take advice.
- He will need to have demonstrated patience.
- Confident – A man who believes in himself and knows what he wants.
- Has respect and moral integrity – both partners have to treat each other with respect for each other's opinions, careers, interests, friends, bodies and minds through their actions.

Here are some of her traits that can make her wife material:

- **Supportive** - to give help or assistance or to hold something or someone up.
- **Cooperativeness** - working or acting together willingly for a common purpose or benefit.

For the Streets/Can't Take Seriously - She is the most common type of woman you will meet and the least recommend to take seriously.

She is the product of a broken home. Who was raised solely by a bitter mother? Who kept the father away? She is the mother of Pookie, Ray-Ray and Simp. Who does not want her children to do better than herself? She never talked to her children about her past mistakes. Never talked about how to do better. She will instead double down and poison her daughter against men. At the same time, teaching her son how to Simp. She will have had multiple children from different men. She will be the most masculine of the three. She will be the most enamored with making money because money was always lacking in her household. She will be cold to have a relationship because she has never seen nor experienced a true feeling of support or attachment. It will be very hard for her to trust anyone because, from her experience, trust was never earned. She is not able to take advice because she will always take it as a personal attack instead of constructive criticism. She is the most rebellious. She will always work against her best interest because she is an emotional wreck. She is the most damaged because no one has ever been able to reach over the walls that she has created.

Her traits:

- **Argumentative** – having or showing a tendency to disagree or argue with other people in an angry way.
- **Need to be right** – a coping mechanism to protect you from others getting close or from feeling not good enough.
- **Lacks accountability - when** someone does not take ownership of an unproductive situation that results from their own actions and subsequent choices.
- **Lacks responsibility** - Lacking interest in their work and in the wellbeing of the team. Blaming others for mistakes and failures. Missing deadlines. Avoid challenging tasks and projects, and do not take risks.
- **Selfish** - lacking consideration for others; concerned chiefly with one's own personal profit or pleasure.
- **Unappreciative - not** fully understanding, recognizing, or valuing something.
- **Shaming** - a painful feeling that's a mix of regret, self-hate, and dishonor.
- **Combative** - aggressive and eager to fight or argue.
- **Disrespectful** - to act in an insulting way toward them. When you disrespect people, you think very little of them. Disrespect is all about not showing respect. Actually, it's about showing the

opposite of respect by acting rude, impolite, and offensive.

- **Uncaring** - lacking proper sympathy, concern, or interest.
- **Self-absorbed** - overly concerned with yourself, including your own feelings and thoughts, you're self-absorbed. Self-absorbed people don't think much about how others are feeling. Your self-absorbed acquaintance Isn't likely to ask you sincerely how you're doing today because he's too busy thinking about themself.
- **No self-respect** - A person with no self-respect has no self-worth. She allows herself to be dominated or tossed about by others. They feel important running errands for others. It's not necessarily a helpful nature, but that's how they see themselves as important.
- **Vain** - excessively proud of or concerned about one's own appearance, qualities, achievements, etc.; conceited: a vain dandy. Proceeding from or showing pride in or concern about one's appearance, qualities, etc., resulting from or displaying vanity.
- **No values** - People live their lives without caring for a lot of things and without meaning.
- **Low self-esteem** - when someone lacks confidence about who they are and what they can do. They often feel

incompetent, unloved, or inadequate. People who struggle with low self-esteem are consistently afraid of making mistakes or letting other people down.

- **Arrogant** - exaggerating or disposed to exaggerate one's own worth or importance, often in an overbearing manner.
- **Fake** - a person who is not genuine.
- **Obsessive** - Obsession is a feeling of intense infatuation, while love is rooted in mutual care and support. Someone who is obsessed with their partner often sees them as someone who needs constant protection and monitoring.
- **Toxic Femineity** - the adherence to the gender binary in order to receive conditional value in patriarchal societies. It is a concept that restricts women from being cooperative, passive, sexually submissive, gentle, and deriving their value from physical beauty while being pleasing to men.

She is looking for:

Pookie, Ray - Ray or Bad Boys for life. These types of men are best suited to deal with this type of woman because she is actually a good reflection of his home life growing up.

CHAPTER 6

THE STRONG AND INDEPENDENT ERA

What does being strong and independent mean?

For a woman, it means:

· That you are able to find happiness on your own. You have self-confidence without having to rely on another person or society for validation. It means emotional independence and being able to have healthy relationships with others without falling into co-dependent patterns.

For a man, it means:

· They don't use other people and don't allow themselves to be used. They are excellent at setting and enforcing their boundaries. They know when to say yes and how to say no. Becoming this kind of person takes a lifetime, and a strong and independent person is always involved in self-help self-growth activities.

Ok, so now that we have a clear definition of what it means. Let's explore what these terms actually mean when applied in the real world.

When I read the definition of a strong woman, it made me laugh. Why? It is because the definition is actually counter to their nature as women. A woman's nature is to be emotional. The first part is "That you are able to find happiness on your own." This is a basic human fact. No one can make you happy other than yourself. So, how is this a flex? Next, "You have self-confidence without having to rely on another person or society for validation." It is just restating the obvious: no one can make you happy but yourself. The final statement, "It means emotional independence and being able to have healthy relationships with others without falling into co-dependent patterns." This is just verbal judo. Who are you emotionally independent from? By this definition, it would be from yourself since you are the only one who can control your own emotions. So then, how can you have any type of healthy relationship if you can't even manage your own feelings? Who benefits from this logic? Corporations. If you can detach yourself from your emotions, then the need to create a family will not be there. You will be more submissive to following your boss's instructions. If you are for the streets, it allows you to have sex with multiple men. It allows you to have babies with a Pookie and Ray-Ray. Knowing that he could care less about you or his baby. Isn't this so liberating?

Don't you find it odd that in order for you to feel strong and independent in society, all you have to do is cheapen your self-worth? You think that having a family when you are young hinders you from living. So, tell me, exactly what are you missing out on? The emotional trauma from sleeping around? How does this benefit you as a woman? Oh, my bad, because a man can do it, you want to do it too. You want to act like a men so much that you would copy all of negative traits that you have said you don't like. Yet you want to follow any of his examples of leadership? Make it make sense. Society would have you think that to feel empowered, you should have sex without a commitment. You don't need to have the protective covering of a husband. The only one who would have your best interest at heart. Society would also have you believe that you don't need a husband. After all, you have that government check and child support. Having a husband could never be as fulfilling as working a corporate job.

You would rather:

- Work a 40-hour work week plus overtime.
- Have as many children as you want by different men.
- Get on child support because having a husband is too restrictive.
- Work to support a childcare provider since you don't have the time to be a mother.
- You enjoy listening and following your boss direction because he cares for you more than a husband ever could.

- Make that bag even though it will be empty because you have all of these expenses and responsibilities with no help in sight
- You don't need a husband because you ain't no body slave unlike your corporate boss.
- You don't need to be supportive of a husband when you can support your boss in making their deadlines.
- You don't mind being stressed emotionally and financially from your job is more rewarding then having a husband who can help you ease your burden .
- Why have a husband who can split the bills and responsibilities? Who has a personal investment in you and his family?

I know why you feel this way. It's because you know the type of man you can get. He is not the type who can provide you with security. This is what your empowerment has gotten you. Great job. You are acting more and more like a man each and every day. Guess what you will also get the same results as a man not being able to find someone to marry.

You have lowered your value as a woman by abandoning your natural nature to become a corporate tool. It is not a societal norm that you are raging against. You are raging against your own human nature.

For the men, have you noticed how the definition of a strong man almost matches that of a traditional man? They don't use other people and don't allow themselves to be used. They are excellent at setting and enforcing their boundaries. They know when to say yes and how to say no. Becoming this kind of person takes a lifetime, and a strong and independent person is always involved in self-help and self-growth activities.

Notice in contrast to women, men are actually working within their nature. While women are encouraged to work against them, there are. Men are providing what men have always provided since creation. Nothing has really changed except that now, these values are demonized by men and celebrated by women.

CHAPTER 7

CAN MEN BE FRIENDS WITH WOMEN?

First, there is a difference between male friends and female friends.

A male friend:

- You can call to help you move because he has the strength to help carry the heavy load.
- A male friend you can call when you are having a problem with your car because he may have tools that you could borrow to fix your car.
- A male friend can give you dating advice because he wants you to score.

A female friend:

- A woman can help you dial AAA because she is not about to get her nails dirty.

- A woman friend can just watch and when the work is finished help you unpack.
- A female friend, depending on her level of pettiness, will give you bad advice because she doesn't want another woman to ruin her good thing.

Now, I know this does not apply to all women, just some. There are some women who seriously are not interested in you, and you are not in them, but still when you think about it. Over the years, you have provided her with more husband privilege than she has a friend. Think about it: Whose friendship have you benefitted the most from? I'll wait.

CHAPTER 8

THE FRIEND ZONE

The dreaded Friend Zone. This is the zone where all good men are shelved. They are in the emergency break glass box that is to be broken only when needed. It is normally broken when she is in her thirties and has children outside of marriage. She will break this box after the man she wants no longer wants to deal with her. So, she is looking for that validation that she was not the problem.

In steps the simp, he will be there to comfort her. He will tell her all the things that she wants to hear in trying to gain favor with her. He will feed her ego. He will tell her that she did nothing wrong and that her ex was the one with the problem. He will tell her that she is so special and does not deserve to be treated like this. He will take her out to dinner and pay to get her nails and feet done. He will step in to help with her children, trying to show how helpful he can be. Hoping that she will choose him as her next choice.

If you are in this box, then it is your fault. If you don't have the self-confidence to accept that she is not interested in you and will, in most cases, only see you as a backup plan. Well, then you do you. My advice to everyone else is to let the fantasy go. Yes, you can still keep her number, but unless you are friends with benefits (which you are not because you are in the friend zone). Why would you ever feel the need to call her? She is not your friend. She is a user. I know you will say no, dude, but you are wrong we have been friends for years. Yes, I can agree that there are some who could really be friends, but that is not the majority. No, my friend, you have been her friend. She has never been yours.

Now, also within this zone are the good guys. They are not as bad as the Simps. They do know their self-worth. They just can't help themselves to try and come to the rescue of the damsel in distress. They will be the emotional support for them. They would never question how or why they got dumped. Their only concern is to encourage them. Unlike the simp, they will not provide any type of financial support, nor would they entertain the idea of helping them with their children. They understand that they have boundaries that they will not cross. In most cases, both the simp and the good guy are hoping that she will choose them as her next choice, but she will never take either of them seriously. Now, some good guys could get the benefit of being her maintenance man.

· *Maintenance man* – Someone who does not

have any emotional attachment but can have an intimate relationship.

This is actually the best position to be in because at least you have a stronger relationship than most. So, you are really good friends with the ability to meet new people, with no judgment. She is not expecting anything from you other than an intimate relationship every now and then until she can find her steady friend.

CHAPTER 9

THE DATING SYNDROME

There used to be a time when there was no such thing as dating. When children came of age, their parents would make the arrangements for them to marry, and that was that. The children were notified of the marriage arrangement, and then with the parents nearby would watch the children as they got to know each other. There was no sex before marriage. You were barely able to kiss before marriage. This was the tradition for most of history. It wasn't until the 20th century that things started to change.

Now, when I say change, I mean for the Western world. In other countries outside of Europe and America women are still performing their traditional role as the main person who takes care of the house and children. They have very few relationships before marriage. They are taught the value of traditional marriage and being a wife. They understand the role of a man as the main breadwinner. His wife's main role is to raise the children and maintain the house. She was not brainwashed by Western ideas.

A lot of men and women in the Western world are not raised in a traditional home. They did not have a nuclear family.

· **Nuclear Family** – a couple and their dependent children, regarded as a basic social unit.

They were denied that example of a healthy household due to feminism. Now let me be clear: there are levels to having a healthy household. You could have the leader father, or you could have the submissive husband. The leader's father is a man who fits the traditional man model. The traditional man would have been married to only one wife and raising only his children. At the same time, the submissive man fits the model of the traditional wife. I am not throwing shade at anyone. I am just pointing out the obvious: not all men are created equal.

CHAPTER 10

THE BROKEN FAMILY

So, when there is no strong male role model in the home, who do you think the sons and daughters are learning from? Yes, the mom. She is the first teacher in their life. The first woman in his life. She is the model that her son will model all women against. She is the role model that her daughter will try to copy. She is the example that will instill the concepts of relationships. She will be the one to instill the benefits of being either a married couple or a single mother.

So, ladies, you are the main reason why men are the way that they are. You raised them to be that way. They don't know how to be the man you want because he was raised by a woman. He learned about manhood from the guys you brought home. So, then, where does the daughter learn how to pick a good man? She looks to her mother, her aunties, her grandma, Hollywood and social media. Now, if she is for the streets, then the men she introduces her son and daughter to are more than likely a Pookie and Ray-Ray or Simp.

We are living in a time where men are blamed for everything from being an unfit father to being dusty and having no ambition. The sad truth is that for some of us, we have earned this title. Now, let us not forget who gets to choose who they have sex with. Let's not forget who raised us to think this way. Who are the gate keeper to sex? Who is the one who has multiple types of contraceptives that can be used before and after having sex? Who screams my body my choice until the choice does not benefit them? Yeah, I know accountability and responsibility is a bitch.

Men are told that it is ok to be just average. It is ok to just do you. We are told that the reason why you haven't reached your goal is because of racism or bigotry or quotas or whatever. Now, this is true in some cases, but the truth for the ones to whom this applies is that you are lazy. You were never taught how to work for what you want. You were never shown how to strive to become better. You were only shown how to take the easy way out. There once was a time in our society when a man would have gotten offended in seeing a woman working harder than himself. Now we are just looking to women to fill in the gaps. You should be ashamed of yourself that a woman is more masculine than you. I am not speaking to all, just a select few, because, as we all know, bad apples get the most attention. However, the real question is why she is picking the bad apples.

Hmmm, could it be because she is not qualified to be with a good man?

Well, for the men who want to change, here are some suggestions on how you can become the better version of yourself:

- The first thing you should try to do is work on your physical appearance. When was the last time you went to a gym?
- Are you working in a career that can allow you to make six figures?
- Do you smoke or drink? If more than socially, then stop. It is not attractive. It also does not show a sense of confidence but of weakness.
- You need to work on your general appearance. I understand that you are working hard and don't feel the need to buy the latest trend in fashion. But you can upgrade your style. You need to develop your own sense of style that separates you from the rest.
- Wear a nice watch; this gives the appearance that you are a man who is about business.
- Finally, you need to start wearing colognes, which is a major draw. Women are sensual. So, if you smell good, they will always be curious about you.
- Work on your social skills.

When was the last time you thought of someone other than yourself? Have you ever attempted to help someone out just because they needed a helping hand? Example: You have a friend who is looking for a job but won't tell him that where you are working, they are hiring. You won't tell him because it doesn't benefit you. Example: You won't encourage your friend when he has lost his job due to no fault of his own. You would rather say damn, dude, that's tough instead of saying dude, let me ask around and see what we can find. When was the last time you gave advice to help someone who was not related to you? Example: You have a co-worker who told you about this great investment, and after you have looked into it, you realize, yes, this is a great investment, but you won't tell another soul because it's all about you.

If you are selfish, how is that an attractive character trait to a woman? Hell, how is that cool with anyone? Now, don't get me wrong. You will still be able to get a girlfriend, but stop shooting for the stars when you don't even qualify for the basic.

You need to see yourself as a conqueror of problems, not as a victim of bad decisions. This applies to both men and women. There is no such thing as a bad decision, only lessons learned. Remember when you used to just shrug your shoulders when things got tough? Where is that person now? That person is still there inside of you. Let that person out. That person that you see in the mirror each and every day. Why are you caging that person in? You are better than this. You are not a beer commercial; you are not a thot for the streets. You are a hard worker who has never allowed anything to ever stop you from achieving. So why start now? Do you think this weakness is attractive? Do you think any person would be able to see a future with someone who sees no future for themselves? You can do better. Stop having a pity party and do something to change.

CHAPTER 11

———————

THE INTERVIEW

For myself, I had to change how I viewed dating. I needed to really think about what qualities I was looking for and stick with it. I did not want to repeat my same mistakes. So, I decided to treat dating like a job interview.

Yes, I know this sounds crazy, but hear me out. Here are categories:
   1. HR.
   2. Job posting.
   3. Phone interview.
   4. In-person interview.
   5. You give an offer letter.
   6. 90-day probation.
   7. You have the job.
   8. Six-month review.
   9. After six months to a year, then start considering her joining management.
   10. VP position filled.

Now, my technique is really not a new idea. We already do it, but on a subconscious level. Here is the breakdown.

HR

This would be the dating app in which I could scroll through profiles (resumes) to see who I was interested in. You could also have the walk-in (some you meet in passing).

Job Positing

I had to fill out a profile (job description). What were my interests and hobbies (job skills)? What type of qualities I was looking for (my ideal candidate)? I had to explain why I felt like I would be a good fit for someone (company history). I had to describe what a day with me could look like (the job description).

The Phone interview

This is the time in which we would exchange phone numbers and start to have a general conversation in getting to know each other. I would use this time productively. I would ask the questions that I knew would be my deal breaker. (Not qualified for the position). Now, if you still pursue them and it doesn't work out, then guess what? YOU were the problem. YOU knew they weren't qualified.

I have five questions that I normally ask. I will only share one though. LOL Each question is designed to see what type of person they are. One of my question that I always ask is: Have you ever been married? – in asking this question, I am seeking to find out:

- Has anyone else thought they were marriage material?
- If so, then what happened, who called it off, and what was the reason?
- If they say that it was a mutual decision, then I know not to take it seriously because if they are not willing to admit their faults. You will always be to blame for everything instead of looking into the mirror. I am not letting it go any further because I do not want feelings to come into play and cloud my judgment. Since we are still in the getting-to-know-you phase, I don't owe you an explanation. I can just walk away. [APPLICATION REJECTED]
- If they say that we had our faults, then they are worth the effort of getting to know more about because they are aware of their mistakes. [GREEN LIGHT] [PROCEED TO IN-PERSON INTERVIEW]
- How many children do they have if the youngest is under the age of 16[RED FLAG] [APPLICATION REJECTED]? My personal preference is that I don't want to be a step-father.
- Where are the children from the marriage? If while married, then there is no real problem. I still would consider the age of the children because of my preference of wanting not to be a stepfather. If they never married and

have children under the age of 16[RED FLAG] [APPLICATION REJECTED]. They did not demonstrate that they are not still ill responsible. Now, I would consider the application if the youngest is 16 or older because this would have shown that she has become more responsible. [GREEN LIGHT] [PROCEED TO IN-PERSON INTERVIEW]

- If they say I have never been married, then consider their age. If they are over the age of 40 and no one has considered them marriage material, or they say that they turned the marriage proposals in, then [RED FLAG] [PROCEED WITH CAUTION]. This is a strong indicator that they may be hard to deal with.
- If they have never been married but have one child around the age of 16 and around 10[RED FLAG] [APPLICATION REJECTED]. They have not demonstrated that they are not still ill responsible.

Notice that my questions are very structured. This only applies if you are looking to be in a serious relationship. Now, keep in mind this is my preference. Your preference may be different. The whole point of my example is that if you don't know what characteristics you are looking for, then why are you mad at them for YOUR problem? While I was on dating apps, I used to keep 10 ladies in my DM at a time. This was so that I could better manage who I was talking to while interviewing. After seven years, only three people made it past the phone interview.

In-person interview

Ok, so now, after we talked on the phone, my questions have been answered to my satisfaction. We now need to see if there is any chemistry. This is the time that I can evaluate and see if she can be a team player or selfish.

During the interview, we can have a relaxing conversation. See if our views are aligned. Our conversations should be more than just surface-level. If we cannot have deeper conversations, then what are we doing? Our conversations should be deep enough that we can get to see your personality. Now, it is totally up to you if you want to just keep her resume on file [FRIENDZONE] until you find someone you are looking for. I would NEVER advise the friendzone, but that is just me.

You give an offer letter

Now, after the interview and everything went well. You are into each other, and you feel the feeling is mutual. You now ask if they want to date. If they say yes, then your offer letter was accepted. Cool, congratulations (your position has now been filled). Now, the real work begins.

90-day probation

During this time, you need to see if they are

selfish or selfless. See if they are willing to offer and take you out. It doesn't have to be anything big. This is very important because if they do not offer, then they could be showing you that they really are not interested in you. They are more interested in what you can provide them versus wanting to build with you. [RED FLAG] [FAILED PROBATION] They are for the streets, and you are being played.

Now, if they make suggestions on planning for the evening and even paying for it, guess what? Then you have hired a really good candidate. She could be a keeper. Congratulations. Now you can relax a little bit. Enjoy each other's company. There is no need for you to be as on guard if you have followed the other steps. No one is perfect. You still need to take this time to have open communication, but by this time, you should have already aired out all of your concerns (you both are adjusting to each other).

Six-month review
Wow, time has flown by. You have now gotten to know each other. You have had a chance to see their family, friends and vacations (business trips) together. You now know their likes and dislikes. (Their work ethics). This is the time you need to reflect on what you have now learned about them. Were they lying about how they were presenting themselves (resume) to you when you guys first met? Have you found out that they love to argue? Have they shown you that they are not willing to follow your leadership or consider your advice?

Have they been disrespectful? These are the traits you should have been looking out for during this time together. If you haven't been paying attention or excusing these actions, then don't get mad at them. You are the problem because you allowed it. You should have checked them at the beginning of these signs. [RED FLAG] [SORRY YOUR SERVICES ARE NO LONGER NEEDED] They are for the streets.

After a year, they start considering them to join the management

Look, let's stop playing games. If you have been with them for longer than a year and no red flags have been shown, then you may have found the one. You need to let them know what your expectations are now [YOUR YEARLY REVIEW]. Are you considering them for marriage or not? (VP position) You should have had this conversation around this time. If not, then why waste their time? Don't give the bullshit reason that I am still not sure. You are sure you are just being insecure and keeping all of your options open. Now I am not saying, I repeat, I am not saying that you should get married after a year. What I am saying is that you should be married-minded by now.

Now, if you have had this conversation and they do not want to be married but want to be in a committed relationship with you [SHE LIKES BEING AN EMPLOYEE], then you have struck gold. Marrying in this day and age is not for the weak. If they do say they would like to get married, then I would strongly suggest getting a prenup. If they say that they do not want to sign one, then I am sorry. You have wasted your time with them. This is the final sign that shows that they have been using you all this time. [RED FLAG] [BREACH OF CONTRACT] I am sorry that it has taken you almost two years to find this out, but it is always best to find out now before it costs you your life savings. (BANKRUPT YOUR COMPANY). Now, if you have missed all of the signs and are getting married without a prenup, then I wish you all the best. If you are a guy, be aware that a woman already has her prenup in place. It is called divorce court. The judges are already on her side. So are the family courts. So, by getting a prenup, all you are doing is balancing the playing field.

You need to be wary and not become the Starter husband.

· **Starter husband** – is a brief first marriage between two young adults, regarded as preparation for subsequent, longer–lasting marriages with different partners.

Guys, you find this type of type of marriage common with celebrities, professional athletes or high-earning professionals. These types of women are usually from the streets. They are always looking to get money with little effort. You can usually tell them apart from the other types of women because they are the ones who you never see in their natural hair, nails, or eyelashes. They will rush to get a Brazilian butt lift (BBL) and swear it is not to get a man but for themselves. If this is really true, then my sisters, you need to get therapy. You were beautifully created naturally. Most men would never take a woman who wears the extra enhancement seriously for a long-term relationship. Now, as previously stated. You will always have guys who will want to play with you. Hell, if your game is good, you may even be able to get a baby from them. Girl, if you can make that happen now, you have secured the bag for at least eighteen years. The more kids you can get out of him the better. Now, if this is your goal, then don't you dare talk about your man cheating.

CHAPTER 12

CHEATING

I had a fun conversation with a friend. I had just told her that I was writing this book on dating. She said good. You better talk about these cheating men out here. I was like, you know what, that is a good topic. Here we go.

· *Cheating* – when a person in a monogamous romantic relationship has an emotional or sexual relationship with someone else without their partner's consent.

I love it when people use this statement because it is a loaded and triggering word. Everyone wants to blame the other person. I say look in the mirror, and that is why the other person did what they did.

Why do men cheat? The primary reason why men cheat is because he was in a vulnerable position that has been building over time. Now, let me be clear. I am only talking about the good guy, not the other examples of men. I am only talking about the guys who value loyalty. Suppose you decided to marry Brad, Chad,

Pookie, or Ray-Ray. What were you thinking was going to happen? These men were cheating on you before you got married or started dating. Hell, he was cheating on his wife or girlfriend to be with you. So quite crying the victim.

The good guys are the type of men who will do everything they can to make a relationship work. So, what happened? What made this guy do something that is against his nature?

- Being disrespected – to act in an insulting way toward them.
- Unappreciated – Not being recognized for how good or important they are.
- Being emasculated – the act of belittling, demeaning or undermining a man's masculinity.

Any one or a combination of these three can cause a good man to be vulnerable to cheating. Now, let's be crystal clear. Only woman controls access to sex. Men control the access to relationships. So, this is how it more than likely happened. He has a female friend who was in his friend zone. She realized after he found someone that she messed up on letting a good guy go. So, she uses her role as a confidant to fill all of the roles that his girlfriend or wife wasn't. Now, over time, she has been showing him what she wanted him to see. He starts to get closer to her. The relationship that he had with his girlfriend or wife continues to deteriorate. She has continued to do one of the three things that has been pushing him away. Now, during a moment of weakness, he succumbs to her manipulation. This could have been a one-night stand, or it could have developed into a full-blown relationship. Yes, he was at fault. He was the one in a committed relationship. He also was not getting his desires met by the woman whom was supposed to be committed to him.

Now, when a woman cheats, it is a lot worse because she is the one who controls the access to sex. A woman cheats as a matter of convenience.

She will cheat because:
1. She is bored.
2. She has lost interest.
3. She wants more excitement.
4. She feels restricted.
5. She feels neglected.
6. She feels underappreciated.
7. She could be listening to her jealous girlfriends.
8. She feels insecure.
9. She got the idea from social media.

Women act off of their feelings. This is why women are not taken seriously by men when they say their man cheated. A woman cheats not just because she finds the other guy appealing. She can cheat just because she feels like she is getting back at him. This is truly an emotional response that really doesn't make sense. Do you think that breaking your values is going to make you seem more valuable or that you will be able to get him back once he finds out? Yeah, you really are for the streets. Now, don't get me wrong, I am not condoning the actions of either party. I am pointing out that a man would have to have put in a lot of work to be able to attract another woman. He would have to have demonstrated that he is a great catch. You don't necessarily have to be that attractive as a woman to get a man. You just need to be willing to perform the act. So don't cry the victim.

CHAPTER 13

SHAME, INSULT AND THE NEED TO BE RIGHT

Ok, now let's talk about this. I don't know if this has always been the case, but have you guys noticed that you cannot have a real conversation with a woman anymore? What do I mean by that? Well, let's say that you and a young lady are having a conversation. It starts off as a really good conversation. You both laugh and tell jokes and then she asks you how you feel about whatever. You tell her your true thoughts, but because she doesn't agree with you now, the verbal judo begins. She begins by telling you how your views are wrong or that you do it too. She starts saying your views are misogynistic. So, when you start to defend your view with well-documented evidence on the topic. She argues that is not true, so you ask her for her evidence. She then goes on to say that she has a friend or just doesn't want to believe in what you are saying. So, the only reason why she is right is because her feelings do not allow her to be wrong.

So why am I bringing this up? Because in the

dating world I run across this all of the time. A lady would ask me how I feel about my dating experience, and she would automatically say you're wrong. So, I then ask how many you have dated? They normally then follow up by saying she probably did say that because of whatever. You should have just let her have her way. I just laugh it off and then say. So, my opinion means nothing in a conversation if you don't agree with it. LOL [RED FLAG] [APPLICATION REJECTED] Girl, bye.

Talking with some ladies is like talking to a child. Suppose they can't have their way. They will throw a temper tantrum. Now, I know that I am not the only guy who has had this experience. Now, for all of the ladies who may be reading this. I know that you are triggered. I know you are screaming, but men do it too. Well, my statement to that is yes, this could be true, but not to the degree that women do. In the social media world, you have whole podcasts created just to shame men and have over 100K subscribers. This is so cringe. You also have the simps who will also co-sign on this narrative. They do it because they are trying to get clicks and views from women. So basically, women who don't like men are blaming men for being men. Yet, if they could attract the man that they want. Guess what they would not have a word to say. I wonder why?

How do you think this is going to work out? If you have the mindset that all men or woman are trash? The problem is not with the other person.

The problem is with you. You are the only common denominator in all of your relationships.

You would rather spend all of your energy talking down on men instead of listening to them. This is crazy. You do realize that men are also watching your social media feeds and podcasts. We are all listening to how you feel about us. We know that there are a few who don't really mean what they are saying but do so for the likes and subscribers. I get it. It's all about getting the bag. I can see that you have not really thought this all the way through. The men in your area know who you are. The men who are not in your area can see your face. Now they know how you feel about men in general. You have quite literally blacklisted yourself from any chance of being with a good man. Hell, even the Simps are not going to want you, and that is saying a lot. Just kidding, a simp doesn't care. LOL.

You have now globally put it out there that you don't give a damn about the cares or wants of men. You only care about you. Do you think men are not paying any attention? It's one thing to say these things on the radio, because at least we cannot see what you look like. You could always deny that you said it. You can't do that on a webcast, not only that. Your future children will see how their mom acted when she was younger. Do you not understand how much shame you are placing not only on yourself, your family and also your future family? I know that you couldn't have thought this through. Well, it's all right. We hear you and accept what you say. I have said it earlier.

Your criticism is dually noted. If any man defends this type of criticism, then you are not just a simp. You are an ultra-simp. You are the lowest of the low. Why? Because you will have demonstrated that you have no self-respect at all. Don't you know that by pandering to them, you are not winning points with them? You still won't be any more attractive to them. Your podcast will not blow up. You may accidentally do something that may go viral, but trust and believe it was an accident. No one cares about a person who has no self-respect for themselves. Ok, I am sorry. I am back. This topic triggered me.

CHAPTER 14

WHY ARE YOU SO ANGRY?

Ladies, if you are still here, I have a question. Why are you so angry towards men? I mean, seriously, why? You have been screaming at the top of your lungs that you want to be treated equally like men. Now that we have listened and are taking you up on it. Now you are mad that we don't treat you like a lady. You can't have it both ways.

You get on social media and tell the world that you don't need a man. Cool, then stop getting mad now that we don't pay you any attention. We will not approach you in public, at work or anywhere that we see you because you have made it crystal clear that you don't need nor want our attention. We will now only spend our time with women who want to be with us. We don't need to hear your mouth. We don't need to understand your struggles. We don't need to have patience with you while you sort it all out. That is a you problem, not an us problem. You have been bold to tell men that they need to get their shit together and do better. Well, guess what? The guys that you don't want have always been doing just that. I am talking about the good guys. They have been doing this since forever. You wouldn't know that because you have put them in your friend zone. So, your problem is with the Pookie and Ray-Ray, Brad and Chad, whom you have been chasing for most of your life. Now that we have that cleared up. I hate to be a bearer of bad news, but these guys don't give a fuck about what you have to say. You love them just the way they are, and they know it. So why would they change if it has been working so well for them? Make it make sense.

You are angry at Pookie and Ray-Ray because they leave you with the kids. While they are going on about their life. This is not cool, but hmmm, you chose to open your legs to him. You knew he wasn't into you like that. So how is it his fault? Oh, wait, it's because he is a man. Yeah, ok, I am over this. Look in the mirror. So far, all of the things I have pointed out are your problem, not our problem. If you choose better, you will be able to get better. Oh, wait, my bad. No, you can't do better either because of your mouth and attitude. Gee sucks to be you. You have become so unappealing that no one can stand to be around you for longer than a minute. Now, I am not talking about the keeper or even the women who are to play with. They are not having any problems meeting good men to be with. Only you streetwalkers have a problem. Only you get mad when called out on your mouth, attitude, and your lack of modesty.

I am bringing this all up not to shame you but because I am trying to get you to see that you need to stop looking to blame everyone in this world for your bad decisions and actions. You can do better if you become better. Take your own advice that you have been pushing all on men get therapy.

Therapy – a form of treatment that aims to help resolve mental or emotional issues.

There are five types of therapy:

- **Psychoanalysis and psychodynamic therapies**. This approach focuses on changing problematic behaviors, feelings, and thoughts by discovering their unconscious meanings and motivations.
- **Behavior therapy**. This approach focuses on learning's role in developing both normal and abnormal behaviors.
- **Cognitive therapy**. Cognitive therapy emphasizes what people think rather than what they do.
- **Humanistic therapy**. This approach emphasizes people's capacity to make rational choices and develop to their maximum potential.
- **Integrative or holistic therapy**. Many therapists don't tie themselves to any one approach. Instead, they blend elements from different approaches and

tailor their treatment according to each client's needs.

Now, just to be clear, not all therapists are created equal. If you are in therapy for longer than two years, then whoever you are seeing may not be helping you but using you. The other reason could also be because you are not taking therapy seriously. You are just going through the motions just so you can say that you went. You will only get out what you are putting into the session. This is supposed to be a safe space to explore your feelings and emotions. This is your first step into opening up. This is your opportunity to make a positive change in your life. You can start to have a healthy relationship. This is your opportunity to become the best version of yourself. Stop listening to people who don't know what they are talking about. Start listening to professionals who have a track record of helping people in your situation. COME ON, you have to WANT IT. It will not be easy, but it will be worth it. You have tried everything else, and look where it has gotten you. Don't be scared to be happy.

CHAPTER 15

WHY ARE YOU FOLLOWING THE CROWD

Stop following every wretched trend that demeans you and start creating trends that can make your image better. You enjoy the streets so much that you would:

- Rather, take relationship advice from a woman who has three kids by three different men.
- Who is faker than a reality TV show? Then, listen to a woman who is supporting her man and raising her children in a loving environment.

No, wait, my bad, you are doing something. You are buying these fake nails, fake hair, fake lashes and getting BBL. Yeah, that is the ticket. I am sure now you have a long line of men wanting to get in your DM. I am sure your Only Fan's subscription is now blowing up. Congratulations, you have now shown the world where your values are. Look, you can justify your actions however you want to. I am not judging you. The fact is, though, that in the real world, you are looked upon as a 304 (a hoe). Yes, you are making a serious bank now. You are young, in your twenties and thirties, living the good life. Prostitution has always been a big money maker. Now with today's technology, you no longer need a pimp. You can do that for yourself. This is the oldest profession in the world. It doesn't hurt anyone as long as they are legally consenting adults. All of the Simps, Pookie, Ray-Ray, Brad, Chad and bad boys in the world, thank you for the service that you are providing. The only problem, though, is that what you are selling gets old over time. You will soon be competing with the younger version of yourself. You will then start to look for a good guy. The only thing is he won't be there for you. no guy would want to deal with a woman who has no self-respect for themselves. Well, wait, you do have one. They have been waiting all this time for you to notice them. They are called simps. See, there is a man out here for everyone.

CHAPTER 16

YOU CAN NOT PLEASE THEM

BY ROBERT MUGABE

YOU CAN NOT give a woman everything she needs.
If God Himself gave them eyebrows, they shave it and draw their own.
God gave them nails, they cut it off and fixed their own.
God gave them hair, they cut it off and fixed their own.
He gave them breasts, they repackage it to what they want.
God still gave them buttocks. They arrange it to the size they want.
If even God can't satisfy them then who are you to think that you can please them?

My brother doesn't kill yourself.

CHAPTER 17

HERE ARE THE CONSEQUENCES OF IRRESPONSIBILITY

References: <u>Fatherless Single Mother Home Statistics | Fix Family Courts.</u>

Fatherless/Single Mother Home Statistics

Many School Shooters are the Product of Broken Homes.

School shootings have been increasing, and there is a strong probability that this is the product of single-parent homes that are fatherless, the result of a failed social experiment by the family courts. Family courts force children into broken homes with single parents just because the parents divorce or separate, even when both parents are fit.

Broken Homes are Leading to Adolescent Epidemics

The following statistics were submitted by

Paul Clements, a father in this fight, who has shared this compiled research. Much of the research is gender-based because there has been a strong father initiative over the last decade to get fathers back into children's lives after a monotherapy standard (which, by the way, was implemented by mental health workers that the court adopted as the tender years doctrine), this is where the belief was that mother's were better suited for parenting children, which drove gender-biased family court policies like tender years doctrine, and caused the loss of father's in children's lives.

SINGLE MOTHER HOMES Statistics

Single motherhood has grown so common in America that today, 80 percent of single-parent families are headed by single mothers — a third live in poverty.

37.8% of single mothers were divorced in 2004. Now it's 29.3% in 2024. 41% were never married in 2004, now it's 51.4% in 2024. And only 6.5% were widows in 2004, but now it is 3.6% in 2024.

So around half 51.4% of women have never been married out of this number. About two-thirds are white, and one-third are black.

There are a total of 10.89Million Single Parent homes out of this number:

- 79.5% are being led by mothers.
- 31.3% are below the poverty level.

- 45.4% are receiving food stamps.
- 20.8% have been unemployed for an entire year.
- 9.2% have no health insurance.
- 11.2% have not completed high school.

37.8% of single mothers are divorced, 41% are never married, and only 6.5% are widows. Brookings Institute, "Assessing the Impact of Welfare Reform on Single Mothers," Part 2, 3/22/04.

"The strongest predictor of whether a person will end up in prison is that they were raised by a single parent." C.C. Harper and S.S. McLanahan, "Father Absence and Youth Incarceration", Paper presented at the Annual Meeting of the American Sociological Assoc., San Francisco, CA, 1998.

In 1996, 70% of inmates in state juvenile detention centers serving long sentences were raised by single mothers. Wade Horn, "Why There Is No Substitute For Parents," IMPRIMIS 26, NO.6, June, 199.

The proportion of single-parent households in a community predicts its rate of violent crime and burglary, but the community's poverty level does not. Source: D.A. Smith and G.R. Jarjoura, "Social Structure and Criminal Victimization," Journal of Research in Crime and Delinquency 25. 1988."

72% of juvenile murderers and 60% of rapists came from single-mother homes. Chuck Colson, "How Shall We Live?" Tyndale House , 2004, p.323.

"After controlling for single motherhood, the

difference between black and white crime rates disappeared." Progressive Policy Institute, 1990, quoted by David Blankenhorn, "Fatherless America: Confronting Our Most Urgent Social Problem," New York, Harper Perennial, 1996, p.31.

Growing up without a father could permanently alter the structure of the brain and produce more children who are more aggressive and angry. Children brought up only by a single mother have a higher risk of developing deviant behavior, including drug abuse, new research suggests. Dr. Gabriella Gobbi, McGill Univ. and Francis Bamlico, Center for Addiction and Mental Health, published in the journal "CEREBRAL CORTEX."

"(I)n a recent study by the Baltimore-based Annie E. Casey Foundation. Comparing statistics for its Kids Count report, the organization reported that Detroit ranks No.1 in unmarried births among the nation's 50 largest cities. Of the 16,729 babies born in Detroit in 1997, 13,574 were black, 1,679 were white and 817 were Hispanic. Seventy-one percent were born to unmarried mothers. This compared with a state average of 33 percent and a 50-city average of 43 percent."

Detroit is the worst offender on our list of America's most dangerous cities, thanks to a staggering rate of 1,220 violent crimes committed per 100,000. "By Thanksgiving 2012, the city had surpassed the 344 homicides reported in all of 2011. As of Dec. 16, the city had recorded 375 murders."

Single parents make up a third of Wisconsin parents, The Annie E. Casey Foundation reports. And according to a 2009 report from the US Census Bureau, there are approximately 13.7 million single parents across the U.S., with single mothers outpacing single fathers five to one.

Two-thirds of all children murdered are murdered by their mothers. Source: U.S. Dept of H&HS website 'Child Abuse Statistics by Relationship' March 2013.

"Girls raised without fathers are more sexually promiscuous and more likely to end up divorced." Wade Horn, "Why There Is No Substitute For Parents," IMPRIMIS 26, No.6, June 1997.

70% of teen births occur to girls in single-mother homes. David T. Lykken, "Reconstructing Fathers," American Psychologist 55, 681,681, 2000.

86% of American teen births are out of wedlock. Dr. David Popenoe, "The Future of Marriage In America," Rutgers Univ., The National Marriage Project, 2007.

"America has more than twice as many teenage births as other developed nations." Isabel V. Sawhill, to House Committee on Ways and Means, Subcommittee on Human Resources, June 29, 1999.

There are more than 400,000 teen births annually in the US, most of them to unmarried mothers on welfare.

National Campaign to Prevent Teen Pregnancy

The public cost of births to teens 17 and younger is estimated at $7.6 BILLION per year. The children are more likely to be in foster care, less likely to graduate from high school, daughters are more likely to have teen births themselves, and sons are more likely to be incarcerated. Saul Hoffman, Univ. of Delaware.

70% of drop-outs and 70% of teen suicides come from single-mother homes. Wade Horn, "Why There Is No Substitute For Parents," IMPRIMIS 26, N0. 6, June 1997.

70% of runaways, 70% of juvenile delinquents, and 70% of Child murderers come from single-mother homes. Richard E. Redding, "It's Really About Sex", Duke Univ. Journal of Gender Law and Policy, Jan.1, 2008.

Effects of Fatherlessness – Teenage Statistics

- 63% of all youth suicides.
- 70% of all teen pregnancies.
- 71% of all adolescent chemical/substance abusers.
- 80% of all prison inmates.
- 90% of all homeless and runaway children came from single-mother homes.

Bob Ray Sanders, "Hey Y'all, Let's Fill The Hall (Of Fame), Ft. Worth Star-Telegram, Oct. 28, 2007.

Mona Charen, "More Good News Than

Bad?", Washington Times, Mar.16, 2001 (citing Bill Bennett, "The Index of Leading Cultural Indicators: American society at the end of the 20th Century., New York, Broadway Books, 1994).

"Look at the detriment to children and society which comes from sole maternal custody," writes Paul.

Children brought up in single-mother homes are

- 5 times more likely to commit suicide.
- 9 times more likely to drop out of high school.
- 10 times more likely to abuse chemical substances.
- 14 times more likely to commit rape.
- 20 times more likely to end up in prison.
- 32 times more likely to run away from home.

Chuck Eddy, "The Daddy Shady Show", Village Voice, Dec. 31, 2002.

The journal Health Affairs reported a five-year drop in the life expectancy of white females without high-school diplomas. White men without high-school diplomas had lost three years of life expectancy http://prospect.org/article/whats-killing-poor-white-women.

600,000 out-of-wedlock births in 1979.

Patrick Fagan and William H.G. Fitzgerald, "Why Serious Welfare Reform Must Include

Serious Adoption Reform. Heritage Foundation Reports, July 27, 1995.

In 2003, there were 1.5 Million unwed births.

Less than 1% were put up for adoption. Fagan and Fitzgerald (above).

Less than 1% of children born to never-married women were placed for adoption from 1989 to 1995. U.S. DHHS, Child Welfare Information Gateway, "Voluntary Relinquishment For Adoption, Numbers and trends, 2005.

Only 4% of college graduates have illegitimate children, and only 16% of college graduates get divorced, compared to 46% of high school dropouts, who marry in smaller numbers to begin with. Dr. David Popenoe, "The Future Of Marriage In America; "The Frayed Knot – Marriage in America," The Economist, May 26, 2007.

50% of single mothers are below the poverty line, and their children are six times more likely to be in poverty than children with married parents. Chuck Colson, "How Shall We Live," Tyndale House.

85% of homeless families are single-mother families. Barry H. Waldman and Stephen P. Perlman, "Homeless Children With Disabilities," The Exceptional Parent, June 1, 2008 (American Academy of Developmental Medicine and Dentistry).

90% of welfare recipients are single mothers. Jason DeParle, "Raising Kevion", New York Times, Aug. 22, 2004.

Over 30% of families led by single moms are

living in poverty, compared to 16.4% of families led by single dads. Amanda Hess, blogging at: http://www.slate.com/blogs/xxfactor/2013/09/19/.

There were 3 million single mothers in 1970 and 10 million in 2003. U.S. Census, Table FM-2, All Parent/Child Situations, by Type, Race, and Hispanic origin of Householder, 1970 to 2003.

More than one million British children currently live without a father and have no adult male role models, a figure that is rising at a rate of 20,000 per year. In the Manor Castle ward of Sheffield, ENG. 75% of households are headed by a single parent, most commonly a woman. Center for Social Justice(6/2013).

The illegitimacy rate went up more than 300% since 1970. House Ways and Means Committee, Nonmarital Births to Adults and Teenagers and Federal Strategies to Reduce Nonmarital Pregnancies, appendix "M," 2003.

The long-term health effects of broken families were often devastating. Parental divorce during childhood emerged as the single strongest predictor of early death in adulthood. The grown children of divorced parents died almost five years earlier, on average than children from intact families. The causes of death ranged from accidents and violence to cancer, heart attack and stroke. Parental break-ups remain, the authors say, among the most traumatic and harmful events for children.

The Longevity Project, By Howard S.

Friedman and Leslie R. Martin (Hudson Street Press) 0020.

Fix Family Courts would like to point out that the last paragraph of the above statistics should be justified. It is not the divorce itself that is causing the adulthood early death, but the result of the child having a parent reduced to a visitor and that parent's authority stripped from the child, which strips the security and stability from that child that is having the dangerous effect on children. You do not strip millions of children of their fit and loving parents more than a divorce already causes and make these children second-class citizens and expect these children not to show any permanent damaging effects.

Thank you, Paul, for supplying these statistics. There have been many others that have brought these statistics to us in the past as well, Mike Whitney, David Mortimer, Thommy Noodlez, Joe Barrow, and Thomas Fidler, to name a few prominent men going through great efforts to assist parents with protecting their children. There are many parent soldiers out there who were just regular parents who have been hurt in this battle and have become a soldier in this effort to help stop this epidemic from being repeated in the next generation. We thank all of you for sharing with us and coming together to end this practice once and for all.

Growing up without a father in a black family

"After controlling for single motherhood, the difference between black and white crime rates disappeared." Progressive Policy Institute, 1990, quoted by David Blankenhorn, "Fatherless America: Confronting Our Most Urgent Social Problem," New York, Harper Perennial, 1996, p.31.

Effects of the Breakdown of the Black Family

Issue: Children from broken families suffer from a number of negative outcomes, regardless of race or ethnicity. Because black families are the least intact,[1] they tend to experience these consequences more than any other race.

Effects of Single Parenthood

- *Crime.* Boys who grow up without a father are twice as likely to end up in jail than those who come from two-parent families.[2]
- *Behavior.* 85 percent of all children that exhibit behavioral disorders come from fatherless homes.[3]
- *Education.* 71 percent of all high school dropouts come from fatherless homes.[4]
- *Poverty.* In 2011, 12 percent of children in married-couple families were living in poverty, compared to 44 percent of children in mother-only families.[5]

State of the Black Family

- Between 1960 and 2012, the share of black adults ages 25 and older who have never been married quadrupled (from 9 percent in 1960 to 36 percent in 2012).[6]
- In 2012, 72.1 percent of African American children were born out of wedlock.[7]
- Only 17 percent of black 15-17 year olds are living with their married biological parents, while 83 percent have lived in non-intact families.[8]

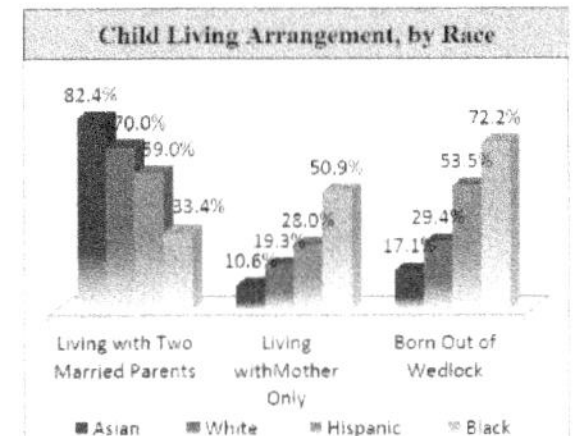

Negative Outcomes for Black Children

- A study by the Progressive Policy Institute found, "After controlling for single motherhood, the difference between black and white crime rates disappeared."[9]

- A longitudinal study of black urban youth revealed when parents were married, adolescents demonstrated significantly higher grades, mediated through paternal involvement.[10]

- The poverty rate for black married-couple families is five times lower than for black non-married families.[11]

Conclusion: The breakdown of the black family has created a multigenerational crisis within the black community. This crisis has not only exacerbated racial disparities, but also has profoundly wounded our nation, especially black children in the next generation.

---

[1] Patrick F. Fagan, "The Fourth Annual Index of Family Belonging and Rejection" MARRI Research, February 2014 available at http://downloads.frc.org/EF/EF14B32.pdf

[2] This figure controls for factors such as income, parent education, race, and urban residence. Cynthia Harper and Sara S. McLanahan, "Father Absence and Youth Incarceration." *Journal of Research on Adolescence* 14 (September 2004): 369-397 accessible at http://www.gwu.edu/~pad202/father.pdf

[3] National Institute of Justice and the Executive Office for Weed and Seed, "What Can the Federal Government Do To Decrease Crime and Revitalize Communities?" National Institute of Justice Research Forum (1998) accessible at https://www.ncjrs.gov/pdffiles/172210.pdf Accessed 3 October 2014

[4] National Institute of Justice and the Executive Office for Weed and Seed, "What Can the Federal Government Do To Decrease Crime and Revitalize Communities?" National Institute of Justice Research Forum (1998). Available at https://www.ncjrs.gov/pdffiles/172210.pdf Accessed 3 October 2014

[5] U.S. Census Bureau. *Children's Living Arrangements and Characteristics.* March 2011, Table C8. Washington D.C.: 2011.

[6] Wendy Wang and Kim Parker, "Record Share of Americans Have Never Married: As Values, Economics and Gender Patterns Change." *Pew Research Center.* September 2014, available at http://www.pewsocialtrends.org/2014/09/24/record-share-of-americans-have-never-married/

[7] Martin J. A., Hamilton B. E., Osterman, M. J. K., Curtin, S. C., & Mathews T. J. (2013). Births. Final data for 2012. National Vital Statistics Reports, 62(9). Hyattsville, MD: National Center for Health Statistics. Available at http://www.cdc.gov/nchs/data/nvsr/nvsr62/nvsr62_09.pdf As cited by "Births to Unmarried Women: Indicators on Children and Youth" Child Trends Data Bank. July 2014 http://www.childtrends.org/wp-content/uploads/2012/11/75_Births_to_Unmarried_Women.pdf Accessed 3 October 2014.

[8] Patrick F. Fagan, "The Fourth Annual Index of Family Belonging and Rejection" MARRI Research, February 2014 available at http://downloads.frc.org/EF/EF14B32.pdf

[9] Progressive Policy Institute, 1990. As cited by David Blankenhorn, "Fatherless America: Confronting Our Most Urgent Social Problem." New York. Harper Perennial, 1996. p.31 http://www.jstor.org/discover/10.2307/2779588?uid=3739936&uid=2129&uid=2&uid=70&uid=4&uid=3739256&sid=21104268888111

[10] Cheryl L. Somers, et al. "Family disruption and academic functioning in urban, black youth." *Psychology in the Schools* 48, 4 (2011): 357-370. Accessed 3 October 2014 Doi: 10.1002/pits.20559

[11] United States. Bureau of Labor Statistics and the Census Bureau. "POV02. People in Families by Family Structure, Age, and Sex, Iterated by Income-to-Poverty Ratio and Race." *Current Population Survey, 2011 Annual Social and Economic Supplement.* Washington: US Census Bureau. 2011. Web. 30 Jul. 2014. http://www.census.gov/hhes/www/cpstables/032011/pov/POV02_100.htm

Many School Shooters are the Product of Broken Homes

School shootings have been increasing, and there is a strong probability that this is the product of single-parent homes that are fatherless, the result of a failed social experiment by the family courts. Family courts force children into broken homes with single parents just because the parents divorce or separate, even when both parents are fit.

Single Mother Statistics

Once largely limited to poor women and minorities, single motherhood is now becoming the new "norm." This prevalence is due in part to the growing trend of children born outside marriage — a societal trend that was virtually unheard of decades ago.

About 4 out of 10 children were born to unwed mothers. Nearly two-thirds were born to mothers under the age of 30. Today, 1 in 5 children under the age of 18 — a total of about 15.7 million — **are being raised without a father**. 1

According to the U.S. Census Bureau, out of about 10 million single-parent families with children under the age of 18, almost 80 percent are headed by single mothers. A third live round half (51.4%) of single mothers have never married, and almost a third (29.3%) are divorced. About two-thirds are White, one-third Black. 2

- Never Married 51.4%
- Divorced 29.3%

- Separated 15.6%
- Widowed 3.6%

Incom

Single mothers earn income that places them well below married mothers on the income ladder. The gap between the two groups is significantly large.

- Single Mothers$51,168
- Married Couples $106,921
- The median income for families led by a single mother in 2021 was about **$51,168**, well below the **$106,921** median for married couples. 6

Poverty

Single mothers are much more likely to be poor than married couples. The official poverty rate for single-mother families in 2021 was:

- 31.3%, nearly five times more than the rate (5.4%) for married-couple families. 7
- Families headed by women of color fared even worse.

- More than one in three (37.4%) of Black female-headed families lived in poverty
- Hispanic (35.9%)
- White (25.0%)
- Asian (19.7%)

Hardship

Families headed by single mothers are among the poorest households:

- Almost a third (24.3%) were "food insecure." 9
- Nearly half (45.4%) received food stamps, while 7.3% received cash benefits from TANF. 8
- In 15 states, TANF benefit levels for a family of three did not even reach 20% of the poverty line, which is equivalent to about $414 per month.

Even for those who did receive assistance, the amount was far less than the minimum they'd need to stave off hardship — like hunger, homelessness, and utility cut-offs.

Access to Health Care

Across all income levels, single mothers are the group more likely to lack health insurance, but the uninsured rates among single mothers have fallen in recent years — thanks to Obamacare.

Access to Child Care

Nationally, the annual cost of center-based infant care averaged over 40% of the state median income for a single mother. About 30% for a school-age child.

In Massachusetts, New York, Washington, Nebraska, and California, a single mother with an infant aged 0-3 would have to pay more than half of her income for daycare at a center.

STATE MOST EXPENSIVE	Average Annual CostFOR SINGLE MOTHER FAMILIES	Cost of CareAS A % OF INCOME
Massachusetts	$21,269	60.4%
New York	$18,574	57.7%
Washington	$19,200	54.5%
Nebraska	$16,640	53.5%
California	$18,201	51.8%

Child care subsidy, if eligible, is hard to come by. In 2021, 13 states had wait lists or had frozen their intake for childcare assistance, with wait times ranging from 90 days to two years. 11

According to the latest available data from the U.S. Census Bureau, 9.2% had no health insurance coverage. 10

Although the Affordable Care Act will give more low-income single mothers access to health insurance, nearly half of these families reside in states that have <u>declined to expand</u> their Medicaid programs.

Among the 11 states not expanding Medicaid coverage, the median eligibility level for parents is just 50% of the federal poverty level, with only two (2) states — <u>Tennessee</u> and <u>Wisconsin,</u> covering parents with incomes at or near poverty.

Access to Education

Single mothers often spend over half of their income on housing expenses and a third on child care, leaving them with less money for educational expenses.

According to the latest data from the U.S. Census Bureau, only 1 in 4 graduated with a college degree, while almost one-sixth had not completed high school. 12

<u>Without financial aid,</u> single-mother students have little or no means to contribute financially to their educational expenses.

Compared to Single Mothers in Peer Countries

The majority of single mothers in the United States are separated, divorced or widowed, and they work more hours and yet have higher poverty rates than single mothers in other high-income countries.

This is due to the fact that many employed single mothers are earning poverty wages in low-wage jobs and often <u>have no access to paid leave</u>.

These, along with less generous "<u>safety net programs</u>" and wage inequality among women, help explain the exceptionally high poverty rate for single-mother families in the U.S.

CHAPTER 18

DIVORCE

The refined divorce rate is often believed to be more accurate.

<u>Divorce Statistics 2023: Everything You Need To Know (grazianolaw.com)</u>

Age plays a significant role in divorce rates. According to the U.S. Census Bureau, younger couples tend to have higher divorce rates, with the risk decreasing as couples age. **The highest divorce rates are among people aged 25-39**.

Interestingly, though divorce rates overall have been declining, the rate for those aged 50 and over (often referred to as "gray divorce") has been increasing.

Statistically, **women are more likely to file for divorce**. A study by the American Sociological Association found that women initiate about 70% of divorces. However, it's important to note that this doesn't reflect the gender distribution of divorced individuals overall, which is more evenly split.

Ethnicity can play a role in divorce rates due

to a variety of socio-economic and cultural factors. According to data from the U.S. Census Bureau in 2021, **African Americans have a higher divorce rate** compared to other ethnic groups, followed by Whites, Hispanics, and Asians.

The Divorce Rate Has Decreased From a Rate of 4.0 to 2.5 Since 2000

Both the marriage and divorce rate have declined over time.

In 2000, a total of 944,000 divorces and annulments occurred. The crude divorce rate was 4.00 per population during that year. By 2021, it had fallen to 2.5 per 1,000 population, with just 689,308 people divorcing that year.

The marriage rate has declined too, dropping from 8.2 per population in 2000 to 6.00 per population in 2021.[1]

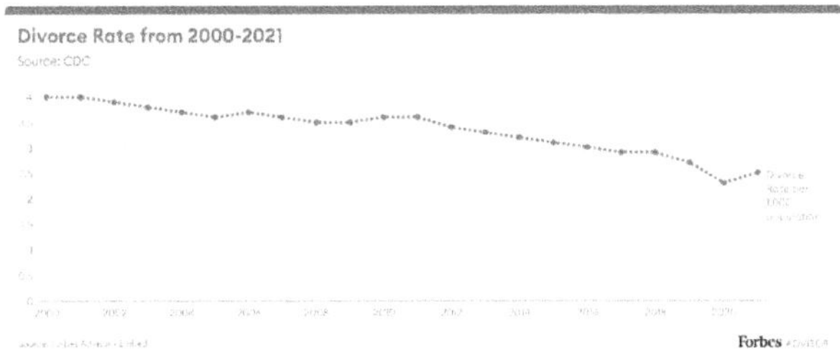

Lack of Commitment Is the Most Common Reason for Divorce

Marriage is not always easy, so success requires both spouses to be dedicated to their union and serious about making it last. That's why it is not surprising that a lack of commitment could spell disaster for a couple.

In fact, 75% of individuals and couples cited lack of commitment as the reason for their divorce. This was the most common cause of a marriage ending, exceeding even infidelity.[2]

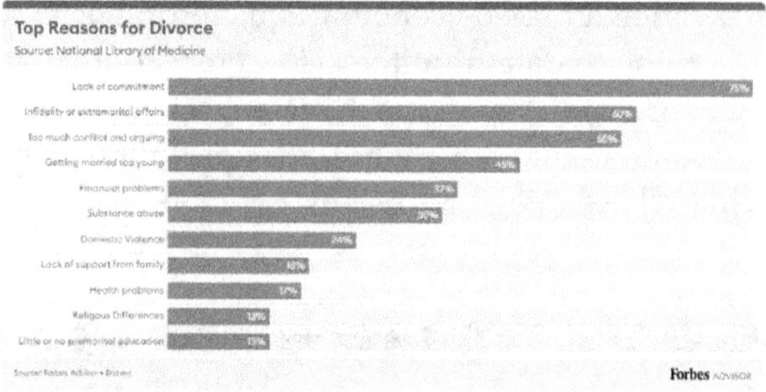

Divorce Rates by Age

Divorce statistics show that each partner's age at the time of marriage can also have an impact on how likely it is the union will last. Couples on both the older and younger end of the spectrum tend to face higher divorce rates.

Couples Who Marry Before Age 32 Experience Lower Divorce Rates

There is a sweet spot in terms of marital age for those looking for the least risk of divorce. That's because couples who marry at 25 are 50% less likely to divorce compared with couples who marry at 20—but for those who marry after age 32, divorce rates increase by 5% per year until the age they are wed.[20]

The Average Age of People Who Divorced in 2022 Is 46 for Men and 44 for Women.

As people grow older, the chance they have ended a marriage increases. In fact, 42% of people between ages 45 and 54 have been divorced. This makes sense as it takes time both to get married and time for the union to fail.[9]

The Median Age of a First Marriage Is Increasing

Many couples have chosen to delay marriage—often for financial reasons or due to changing cultural norms. In fact, in 2022, the median age of marriage was 32 for men and 30 for women.[9]

By contrast, in 2012, the average age for women marrying was 26 and the average age for men was 28. These older marriages could potentially increase the divorce risk if couples are waiting too long to tie the knot and face increased difficulties learning to cohabitate and merge their lives.[21]

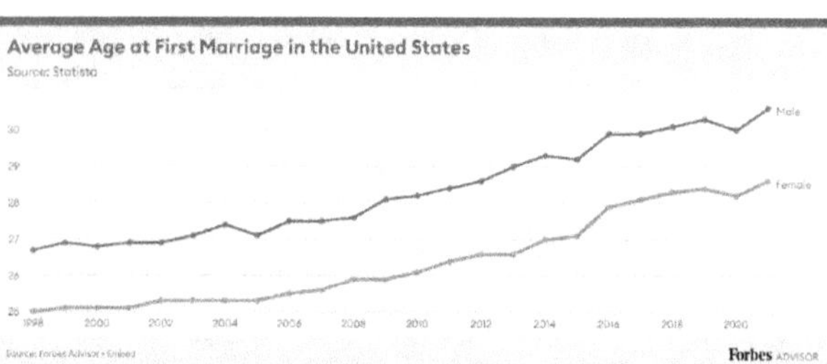

Divorce Rates by Gender

Understanding divorce rates by gender is helpful—especially as this can shed more light on the accuracy of the refined divorce rate. This is the divorce rate measured relative to the number of married women, while the crude divorce rate looks at the number of divorces relative to the population.

69% of Divorces Are Initiated by Women

Women are far more likely than men to initiate divorce. In fact, nearly 7 in 10 marriage dissolutions are initiated by the female partner. This is based on research involving heterosexual couples.[23]

Women often carry more of the mental load in a relationship and also take on a primary caregiving role for children. The added burden they face—especially when they feel their support system is lacking—could help to explain why they are more likely to initiate divorce.

The Divorce Rate for Women Is 7.6 per 1,000 Women Over the Age of 15

In 2019, 7.6 per 1,000 women over age 15 divorced. This is a substantial decrease from 9.7 new divorces per 1,000 women 15 and over, which was the number of divorces among women in 2009.[24]

Divorce Rates by Ethnicity

Divorce rates also vary by ethnicity. Many factors could explain these discrepancies, including differing cultural norms surrounding the institution of marriage as well as systemic biases that undermine family structures in certain communities.

Here's what the data shows about both divorce and marriage rates by ethnicity:

- The divorce rate for white couples is 15.1%. The marriage rate among these couples is 32.1%.
- The divorce rate for Black couples is 30.8%, and the marriage rate is 17.3%.
- The divorce rate for Hispanic couples is 18.5%, and the marriage rate is 33.2%. [25]

Divorce

Education level affects the chances of a marriage succeeding, with those who have attained more education experiencing a reduced likelihood of divorce:

- The divorce rate for people with an education of high school or less is 39% for men and 37% for women.[26]

- The divorce rate for people with an advanced education—defined as having more than a bachelor's degree—is 26% for men and 30% for women.[26]
- 29% of men and 32% of women with a bachelor's degree or higher were divorced in 2022.[9]

College-educated women Are Most Likely to Have a Lasting Marriage

One particular demographic group has the highest likelihood of a long-lasting marriage: College-educated women.

Earning a degree significantly decreases the chances of a woman divorcing. The benefits apply only when the degree is earned, though. Women who attend some college but who do not graduate are far less likely than their credentialed counterparts to remain married over the long term.

In fact, while 78% of women with a bachelor's degree have a marriage that lasts at least 20 years, just 49% of women with some college education reach this milestone. And just 40% of women with a high-school education or less have a marriage that lasts 20 years or more.[27]

US - divorce rate 2021 | Statista

A declining divorce rate

Over the last couple of years, both the marriage and divorce rates have been declining in the United States. As of 2009, the average length of a first marriage in the U.S. was eight years. The average age men were at when they went through their first divorce was 32; for women this was 30. The average length of a second marriage was about 10 years.

Experience, Compassion, Connection.

I WILL BE THERE FOR YOU.

Divorce rate is higher for lesbians than gay men
(friendswoodfamilylaw.com)

The divorce rate is higher for lesbians than for gay men

On Behalf of Jana Landry Attorney at Law | May 14, 2021 | Divorce

When couples in the Texas LGBTQ community marry, they are not thinking of the end of that union. However, they might be interested in the rates of divorce for LGBTQ couples and what data focusing on same-sex couples in England, Wales and Scotland has found.

Divorce rates for lesbians and gays

According to data from the Office for National Statistics, in 2019, 56% of same-sex marriages were between women. However, the <u>divorce rate for lesbians</u> was much higher, with 72% of same-sex divorces in 2019 coming from lesbian couples, about 3 times higher than gay male couples. The lesbian divorce rate was 78% in 2016, 74% in 2017 and 75% in 2018. Interestingly, while same-sex marriages have increased drastically since 2014, when same-sex marriage was allowed in England, Wales and Scotland, the rate of divorce has remained consistent. For most divorces, the reason seems to be "unreasonable behavior," including adultery.

Divorce factors

Considering that marriages between lesbian and gay couples that end in divorce last for similar amounts of years, 4.1 for women and 4.3 for men, it is important to consider the factors that lead to higher rates of <u>dissolution of marriage for lesbians</u>. According to one family law professional, the factors that lead lesbians to divorce are the very same ones that lead women in heterosexual marriages to petition for divorce at a rate about twice as high as men.

These factors include:

- Feeling ignored in a marriage.
- Unequal relationship with one partner pulling the weight in the marriage.
- Adultery.
- Domestic violence.

Ending a marriage is not an easy decision. However, if you find yourself having to make that choice, you should prepare even before you file. Preparation might include gathering evidence and documents related to the marriage and your assets and liabilities and speaking with a lawyer about your options.

Bibliography

1. Table C2, U.S. Census Bureau. Household Relationship and Living Arrangements of Children Under 18 Years, by Age and Sex: 2022
2. Table FG6, U.S. Census Bureau. One-parent Unmarried Family Groups with Own Children Under 18, by Marital Status.
3. Table FG5, U.S. Census Bureau. One-parent Unmarried Family Groups with Own Children Under 18, by Labor Force Status.
4. NWLC. Women in Low-Paid Jobs.
5. PayScale, The State of the Gender Pay Gap in 2021
6. U.S. Census Bureau – Income in the United States: 2021
7. NWLC – National Snapshot: Poverty Among Women and Families.
8. Table C8, U.S. Census Bureau. Poverty Status, Food Stamp Receipt, and Public Assistance for Children Under 18 Years by Selected Characteristics: 2022
9. USDA, Household Food Security in the United States in 2021
10. U.S. Census Bureau - Health Insurance Coverage in the United States: 2021
11. NWLC, State Child Care Assistance Policies 2021
12. Table F2, U.S. Census Bureau. Family Households, by Type, Age of Own Children, and Educational Attainment of Householder: 2022
13. Single Mother Guide 2024 website https://singlemotherguide.com
14. Brookings Institute, "Assessing the Impact of Welfare Reform on Single Mothers," Part 2, 3/22/04

www.ingramcontent.com/pod-product-compliance
Lightning Source LLC
Chambersburg PA
CBHW071448130726
47997CB00006B/2277